Middle-Ag

CU00920976

A Play

Roger Hall

Samuel French–London

New York–Sydney–Toronto–Hollywood

ISBN 978-0-573-11273-7

www.samuelfrench.co.uk
www.samuelfrench.com

FOR AMATEUR PRODUCTION ENQUIRIES

UNITED KINGDOM AND WORLD
EXCLUDING NORTH AMERICA

plays@samuelfrench.co.uk

020 7255 4302/01

Each title is subject to availability from Samuel French, depending upon country of performance.

MIDDLE-AGE SPREAD

First produced in London by John Gale for Lisden Productions Ltd at the Lyric Theatre, London on October 17th, 1979, with the following cast of characters:

Elizabeth	Marjie Lawrence
Colin	Richard Briers
Isobel	Sheila Grant
Reg	Paul Eddington
Judy	Judy Loe
Robert	Tom Chadbon

The play directed by Robert Kidd
Setting by Alan Tagg

The dinner party takes place in July on the last day of the school term, and all the other scenes take place during the preceding weeks

Scene 1	The Dinner Party
Scene 2	Ten weeks earlier—the sitting-room
Scene 3	A few days after Scene 2—Judy's bed-sitter
Scene 4	The Dinner Party continued
Scene 5	Six weeks earlier—the bedroom
Scene 6	A few days after Scene 5—Judy's bed-sitter

INTERVAL

Scene 7	The Dinner Party continued
Scene 8	Three weeks earlier—the sitting-room
Scene 9	A few days after Scene 8—Judy's bed-sitter
Scene 10	The Dinner Party continued

Time—the present

Middle-Age Spread was completed during the writer's tenure of the Robert Burns Fellowship, University of Otago, Dunedin, New Zealand, and was first performed at the Circa Theatre, Wellington, New Zealand on 16th November 1977.

SCENE 1

The sitting-room of Colin and Elizabeth. An evening in mid-July

It is a typical middle-class sitting-room, with no real style but with the emphasis on tidiness and "niceness" rather than being a real place to relax—a room always on show in case people call. (See note on set in Furniture and Property List)

As the CURTAIN *rises the room is empty. Elizabeth enters and places a tray of snacks on the table. She finds a doll—the doll is dressed like a nurse*

Colin enters. He is wearing a smart, brand-new raincoat, and under his arm there is a box of the type suits are carried home in from the tailor's

Colin Sorry.
Elizabeth It's late! They'll be here soon.
Colin Yes, I know. Sorry.
Elizabeth Well, hurry up and get ready—is that a new raincoat?
Colin Yes. I got it tonight—in town.
Elizabeth Well, it's about time.
Colin Do you like it?
Elizabeth Yes, but it's late!
Colin All right, all right.

Colin exits to the hall

Elizabeth goes to the bookshelf and extracts two largish books—one about art, the other on "Raising Daisy Rothschild". She ponders, puts the art book back and places the other "casually" on the coffee-table. A toilet is heard flushing off stage

Colin enters. He is wearing a noticeably new jacket

Elizabeth Did you drip?
Colin What?
Elizabeth On the floor. Did you drip on the toilet floor?
Colin I don't know!
Elizabeth *And* I suppose you used the new bar of soap.

Elizabeth goes out to check; she takes the doll with her

Colin (*pouring two sherries*) No I didn't use the new bar of soap because I was a naughty boy and didn't wash my hands. (*He looks at himself in the mirror, then does the jacket up and holds in his stomach in*)

Elizabeth returns

Well, what do you think?
Elizabeth What?

Colin The jacket?

Elizabeth Good heavens! You have been splashing out.

Colin I needed one. How does it look?

Elizabeth It's very nice. (*She takes a tray and six wine glasses from a shelf and puts them on the table*)

Colin You don't sound very keen. You're sulking because you weren't there to choose it.

Elizabeth No, I'm not.

Colin I thought—just for once—I'd buy something I liked. Anyway, you didn't ask me about those chimes. It's not too short, is it?

Elizabeth It's a bit tight.

Colin Possibly. Don't let me eat too much tonight.

Elizabeth All your jogging doesn't seem to have made much difference.

Colin No. A bit. Hell, I haven't done my Canadian Air Force Exercises today. (*He starts exercising and "jogging on the spot"*)

Elizabeth You haven't got time to start prancing about now! You haven't got the ice ready yet. Oh—and some wine arrived today—it's in the kitchen.

Colin Wine? Oh—*that's* good timing!

Colin goes to the kitchen

Elizabeth sits and drinks her sherry

Colin enters with a bottle of red wine

Colin Look! "Bottled especially for Colin and Elizabeth Wilson." Looks good doesn't it?

Elizabeth Oh yes, that's very nice.

Colin I've put a couple of white in the fridge. What time are they coming? (*He takes a corkscrew from the drinks shelf and opens the bottle*)

Elizabeth I told Judy and Robert seven-thirty, and I told Reg and Isobel seven-fifteen because they're always late.

Colin They can all be late as far as I'm concerned. (*He pours himself a glass of wine*)

Elizabeth Don't start all that again.

Colin You know I didn't want tonight. A man should be able to celebrate the last night of term in the privacy of his own pub.

Elizabeth We've been through all this.

Colin I mean we see Reg and Isobel every other day. And I don't particularly want to meet Judy's husband—why you asked him, I don't know. The only good thing about this evening is the fact that the Hendersons couldn't make it. Here's to a night of wit and reason. (*He drinks*)

Elizabeth If that's what you want, keep Reg off the Scotch. And don't fall asleep!

Colin Me!

Elizabeth The last two dinners we've given you've nodded off near the end.

Colin Well I'm sorry but boredom and exhaustion have that effect on me. I say, is Jane O.K.? I tried her room just now and it was locked. She wouldn't answer.

Elizabeth Just leave her. She's going through one of her anti moods.

Colin That's not like her.
Elizabeth Isn't it! I'm sure I wasn't like that at her age.
Colin I'm sure you weren't.
Elizabeth What do you mean by that?
Colin Elizabeth, your mother wouldn't even have heard of adolescence, let alone tolerate it. I bet you had to eat your greens or no pudding right up until you left home.
Elizabeth Colin what *is* the matter?
Isobel (*off*) Oo-oo!
Colin They're only ten minutes late—they're early.

Isobel enters. She is wearing a long batik dress, leather sandals and has a handbag slung over her shoulder.

Isobel Hallo. We let ourselves in . . . as you can see.

Reg enters

Elizabeth Hallo Isobel, Reg.
Isobel Oh—are we the first? Not like us. Colin! I haven't seen you to congratulate you.

Reg picks up a book and looks at it

Colin Thanks.
Isobel Of course I knew you'd get it. I say—doesn't he look smart! Elizabeth whip you into town?
Colin I chose it myself.
Elizabeth How are you Reg? Glad it's the last day of term?
Reg You could say that, yes.
Elizabeth (*sitting in the swivel chair*) Do sit down.

Reg and Isobel sit on the sofa

Reg How did McIntosh's farewell go?
Colin Oh the usual sort of thing—got his silver tray and a cheque. Gave a rambling speech about moral standards—none of the pupils knew what he was talking about. Miss Reidy cried. (*He tops up his wine*)
Isobel "McIntosh"—I've always thought that a lovely name for a headmaster. What is it the kids called him?
Colin The Plastic Mack. None of us dared wear one you know. He took it as an insult. Now, Isobel—what are we having to drink? There's sherry, beer, gin—vermouth—brandy . . .
Isobel Oooh. Oh—I think just a sherry thanks.

Colin pours Isobel a sherry

Lovely!
Colin Reg?
Reg Scotch.
Colin Oh—er—ah—erm—I'm not sure.
Reg What's this like? (*He holds up his book*)

Colin What?
Reg *The Great Railway Bazaar?*
Colin Very good.
Reg Can I borrow it?
Colin It's not mine.
Elizabeth Yes, whose is that?
Colin Scotch. (*He pours some, opens ice bucket and finds it's empty*)

Colin exits to the kitchen with the ice bucket

Isobel You must be very pleased about Colin getting the job.
Elizabeth Oh yes. He said he wasn't keen to get it, but now that he has, I think he's glad. And I'm glad for his sake, of course.
Reg To say nothing of the money.
Elizabeth It's not that much when you consider all the responsibility he'll have.
Isobel Take no notice of Reg tonight. He's in one of his moods.
A Child (*off*) Mummeeeee!
Elizabeth Excuse me, that's Caroline.

Elizabeth goes out, closing the door

Isobel You behave yourself tonight. I know you didn't want to come—neither did I particularly, but that's no reason to be more boorish than usual. And don't read!

Reg drops the book on the sofa

Elizabeth returns

Everything all right?
Elizabeth Teddy-bear had wind. (*She sits*)
Isobel Oh how lovely! I quite miss her wandering over to our place—how's she liking school?
Elizabeth Loves it.
Isobel And the rest of your tribe—how are they?
Elizabeth Roddy's out at basketball. We let him take the car now he's got his licence.
Isobel Exciting! And how's Jane?
Elizabeth Oh she's locked in her room going through one of her adolescent phases. I presume they do grow out of them.

Reg picks up the "Daisy" book

Isobel I wouldn't count on it. Not if Stephen's anything to go by.
Reg (*commenting on the book*) God, not another book on treating animals as if they were human beings, just because they're a dying species. There's far too much anthropomorphism about.
Isobel Take no notice; it's just his sweeping generalization Number Eighty-seven.
Reg What's so special about a giraffe, for heaven's sake! It's only because the things are photogenic! I mean no-one's ever going to buy a book called

Millicent Mamba or Colin Cobra. I've half a mind to write a book, *My Life With a Newt*. Only it'd invite the inevitable comparison.

Colin comes in with Reg's drink, with ice in

Colin Your Scotch.
Reg No ice, thanks.
Colin Oh. (*He collects his sherry glass, transfers the ice with his fingers, and gives Reg the Scotch*)
Isobel Who else is coming tonight? You did say, but ...

Colin sits on the back of the sofa

Elizabeth That girl Judy I was telling you about—the one who started supply teaching at Colin's school at the beginning of term—she and her husband had split up. Anyway, they're together again now—since I invited her actually—she felt a bit awkward about coming but I insisted. His name's Robert.
Isobel Isn't it lovely to hear of a couple getting together again. These days— I don't know—nobody seems to last. I hear the Watsons are just about ...
Elizabeth Are they?
Isobel So I hear. And that couple who moved in down the road recently— he ran off with someone else while she was in the hospital having their third.
Elizabeth That's terrible.
Reg Isobel has a map of the district on the wall at home. When a couple split up, she pins up a red flag.
Isobel It's not true.
Reg She's like a war correspondent—trying to predict which will be the next to fall—POW! She links it all to the domino theory.
Isobel He's making it all up.
Reg I keep our red flag all ready, just in case. Will Judy keep on teaching next term?
Colin No, she's resigned.
Elizabeth She's got quite a young family.
Isobel And what does he do?
Elizabeth He's an accountant.
Colin Also something to do with Rotary.
Isobel One of Reg's many *bêtes noires*.
Colin Accountants or Rotarians?
Reg Both. Actually I've got a feeling I've met him.
Colin More sherry Isobel?
Isobel Please. I say—you have ice in yours—how trendy.

Colin refills Isobel's glass

Reg I expect it's to go with the jacket.
Colin Reg—how's your glass?
Reg Won't say no.
Colin More for you, dear? (*He refills Reg's glass*)
Elizabeth No, thank you.

The doorbells chime loudly

That'll be them.

Elizabeth goes to the hall

Reg Good God—how long have you had them! I was just about to rush into the street and buy a Mr Whippy.
Colin Elizabeth wanted them. Our front door bell hadn't been working for ages.
Reg Ours doesn't either. Saves a fortune when collectors call for charity.
Isobel Not that he'd give anything if we did hear them. Always got some rationale for meanness. Thanks. Lovely!

Elizabeth enters

Elizabeth Come on through.

Robert and Judy enter

Robert is wearing a smart suit—contrasting with the other men. Judy is less formally dressed than him but quite smart. She is wearing a pendant

Robert, you haven't met Colin have you?
Robert How do you do? Principal elect, I gather, or whatever the term is.
Colin Yes.
Robert Congratulations.
Elizabeth And this is Isobel and Reg—our next-door neighbours—Robert and Judy.
Robert How do you do?
Judy Hi. We have met.
Reg Indeed we have.
Isobel You've taught my son Stephen, I believe?
Judy Oh yes! I like him.
Isobel We don't. Not at the moment, for reasons we needn't go into here.
Judy He's a super writer—does he want to do something like that when he leaves school? It would be a pity if he doesn't.
Reg I think he's got talent—not that I ever tell him that.
Isobel *If* he ever gets the chance to use it.
Colin What would you like to drink?
Judy Gin and tonic, if you have it, please.
Colin We have, yes. Robert?
Robert Same for me, please.
Colin Right. (*He pours and hands round the drinks*)
Robert Nice view you have.
Elizabeth We like it.
Robert I hadn't realized how many nice houses there were up here. What's that big place over there?
Elizabeth Which one?
Robert With the Tudor top storey and the floodlit barbecue.
Elizabeth The Vincents—he's a lawyer. And the place next to it—with the tennis court—is Cooper—you know, the gynaecologist.
Robert Of course, until recently this area's always been undervalued. A client

of mine knew what he was up to—he began buying up houses round here a few years ago.

Elizabeth Lucky man.

Robert Shrewd. Still, you've got to do something like that these days, don't you—just to keep pace with inflation.

Reg Even if it does mean some poor devil paying through the nose for a house.

Robert Well, I'm afraid it's everyone for himself.

Colin Your drink.

Robert Thanks.

Judy Thanks. Hey! I like your jacket. .

Colin Do you really?

Judy Super. It suits you.

Robert I'm sure I've met you before. You're not in insurance, are you?

Reg No, I am not!

Elizabeth He's at Teachers' College—a lecturer.

Reg You came to me once for advice. On Rotary business.

Robert On Rotary business?

Reg About the Wombles Adventure Playground.

Robert Oh yes! Oh yes. You didn't think we should build it. Well, we disregarded your advice I'm afraid—it's almost finished.

Reg I know. I shudder every time I drive by.

Elizabeth I think it's a lovely idea. Why don't you like it Reg?

Reg Because if you stick a whole lot of Wombles or Donald Ducks into the ground—you've taken the imaginative side away from kids. A Womble is a Womble—it can't be anything else—but bits of timber can be anything from a pirate ship to a troll-infested forest. Kids in this suburb need a *real* adventure playground with bits of wood and rope and tools and told to do what they like with it. Not a collection of middle-class statues.

Elizabeth Your idea sounds terribly dangerous.

Robert You'd have to have supervision.

Reg Well, let the Rotarians supervise! Do something useful for a change instead of forcing old ladies into cars on hot afternoons.

Elizabeth Well, I think the Rotarians do a lot of good.

Isobel takes out a cigarette and lighter from her handbag

Reg Only if they're going to be caught in the act.

Judy (*to Isobel*) What a super handbag.

Isobel Do you really think so? I made it myself. (*She lights her cigarette*)

Judy How clever of you.

Elizabeth Isobel's a great one for crafts—she makes most of her own things.

Isobel I made everything I'm wearing tonight.

Judy I wouldn't have guessed.

Isobel Even the sandals. My first effort.

Reg Only cost four times more than a pair from Harrods.

Isobel It's not true.

Judy I must say I admire people who can make all these things. I'm hopeless. Luckily Robert's very practical and does all sorts of things round the house.

Robert I always say if you've done it yourself, you know it's done properly.

Colin Not in my case—quite the opposite.

Elizabeth But you try. You papered the bathroom, remember?

Colin Yes, I tried one of those pre-pasted papers, and I put it in the water, and when I lifted it out I was left with two little bits of paper between my fingers and thumbs. God, I was angry.

Isobel *He* won't lift a finger. Won't even help me with the dishes.

Reg The reason I won't help her with the dishes is that she always keeps hold of the dish when she dips it into the water. I keep thinking of all the germs leaping on to the little Achilles' heel of unwashed plate. And the reason I won't do things around the house is for the same reason that I don't expect painters and decorators to lecture my students. It's a question of professionalism.

Robert What do you lecture in—I've forgotten?

Reg It's called "professional studies"—not that it teaches the students either to be professional or to study. Principles of learning—that sort of thing—whatever's the current bandwagon. At the moment it's open-plan teaching.

Elizabeth Oh, Caroline's in an open-plan class. It can't be good for the children—doing maths on the floor.

Colin I think there's more to open-plan than that, Elizabeth.

Robert It must be an interesting job.

Reg It would be fine if there weren't any students. Trying to get them interested in anything's impossible. Most of them don't even *read*!!

Colin Some survey recently said that there were three and a half million young people in this country who were bored—bored most of the time.

Robert Tch.

Judy It's tragic.

Reg Tragic! It's a crime! The secondary schools are to blame, of course.

Colin Partly. Television—affluence—more leisure.

Elizabeth I always used to play tennis.

Reg How can one be bored when there is still a Dickens to be read, a Beethoven sonata still unheard, a mountain pass still uncrossed? It's this obsession with material things—with personal comfort. Spend your money on your brain—when you're on your death bed it'll be the things you've seen and done you'll look back on—not how much wall-to-wall carpet you owned. We're obsessed with security and investment in this country—look at the Sunday papers! Chock full of schemes to invest in bullion, or stamps, or apostle spoons, to say nothing of unit trusts, endowment plans and pension schemes. *Real* security is coming home of an evening with half of *War and Peace* still unread.

Isobel He says that to all the first years.

Judy I must say I agree with him.

Isobel At home he reads *Biggles* with the electric blanket on.

Judy Oh yes! Super!

Colin I liked Ginger.

Judy Perhaps if kids were forced to study *Biggles* at school, they'd turn to the classics once they'd left.

Elizabeth What *are* biggles?

Reg Oh Elizabeth, you were badly brought up. *Biggles*—every boy's flying hero. I bet you thought they were Jewish rolls you get in New York.
Robert I have to confess I never read *Biggles* either.
Reg Banned at the school you went to, was it?
Robert Quite possibly.
Colin How can you ban anything these days? They can either see it on television or buy it at any bookstall.
Reg So what plans do you have when you take over? How are you going to bring the age of enlightenment to seven hundred pimply adolescents? You must have some ideas?
Colin Reg, the term's just finished, I'm not going to talk shop now.
Elizabeth (*rising*) If you like to get the wine, I'll serve the soup in a minute.
Colin Right.

Colin exits to the kitchen

Isobel He must be pleased, though, about the job.
Elizabeth (*distributing glasses from the table*) I think so. He hasn't said much about it. He had a lot of doubts about even applying for it.
Isobel Oh, but why?
Elizabeth I don't really know.
Judy I think perhaps being headmaster of any secondary school these days is a daunting prospect.
Reg No—he'll have the time of his life.

Colin enters with bottle of white, open, and collects the already opened bottle of red

Colin Red or white? (*He shows the bottles to Judy*)
Judy Red. What's this? "Bottled especially for Colin and Elizabeth Wilson." I say—how snazzy.
Elizabeth It's a good idea isn't it?
Isobel Yes.
Colin It was a special offer in the *Sunday Telegraph Colour Magazine.*
Elizabeth Why don't you all sit at the table. I'll get the soup.

Elizabeth exits to the kitchen

Colin goes round pouring the wine

Isobel Thanks. Lovely.
Robert Red please. They were a good buy those wines—wish I'd bought some now.
Reg White please. (*Looking at the bottle*) Bit've a cock-up with this lot?
Colin What?
Reg Read the label.
Colin Oh no!
Robert What?
Colin "Bottled especially for Metal Box Industries Social Club Welwyn."

Colin sits. The Lights fade to a Black-out, as—

the CURTAIN *falls*

SCENE 2

The same. An evening in May

The room is a bit untidier

Elizabeth, wearing a raincoat, is looking for something. She is in a hurry. She picks up four letters from the sofa table and two from the coffee-table, places them in the main table

Colin enters. He is wearing an oldish raincoat and carries a full briefcase. He goes and slumps on the sofa, exhausted

Colin Greetings.
Elizabeth You're late. Have you seen the car keys?
Colin No. Meeting at school—went on longer than expected.
Elizabeth You had them last.
Colin No I didn't. Did I?
Elizabeth (*continuing her search*) I don't know where they are. Your dinner's in the oven.
Colin I've eaten.
Elizabeth You might have phoned.
Colin I tried. Three times! It was engaged every time.
Elizabeth Oh yes. Jane. I tried to get her off the phone, but she's "in love".
Colin Who with?
Elizabeth I don't know—it seems to change every week. I told her that that was no reason to hog the phone for hours. All she says is, "Mummy, you've forgotten what it's like to be in love".
Colin She's probably right.
Elizabeth Rubbish.
Colin I don't think I can remember what it was like being in love—painful, mainly. I didn't know you were going out tonight.
Elizabeth I told you! You don't listen! It's a cooking demonstration—in aid of the nursery school. Different ways with *fondue*. I don't know where they are—I'll have to get Louise to give me a lift.
Child (*off*) Mummee!!
Elizabeth What can she want now!
Colin I'll go.

Colin exits to the hall

Elizabeth crosses to the phone. It rings before she has chance to dial

Elizabeth Blast. (*Answering*) Hello?... Who?... Oh *yes*!... Dinner Friday week? I think that'll be fine ... Yes. About eightish. Right—thanks. See you then. (*She puts down the receiver and dials. The number is engaged*) Blast.

Colin enters

Colin (*sitting on the sofa*) Did you know Caroline's got that teddy-bear of hers completely bandaged—you can't even see its eyes. Third degree burns, evidently. Bit morbid.

Elizabeth You know how she wants to be a nurse.
Colin Is that why she wakes us at five in the morning? Couldn't we put her to bed later at night.
Elizabeth You don't have to put up with her all day. The Conroys just phoned.
Colin What did they want?
Elizabeth Invite us for dinner Friday week.
Colin Oh no! You know I'm completely clapped out Fridays.
Elizabeth I know! There was nothing I could do. I can't say "We'd love to come, but Colin's always clapped out Fridays". Anyway, you're tired most nights as far as I can see.
Colin True. Any mail?
Elizabeth It's on the table. (*Calling to the hall*) Jane! *You* haven't seen the car keys, have you? What?

Elizabeth goes out to the hall to hear Jane more clearly

Colin opens some of the mail. Two letters are circulars which he tears up. A couple of bills he puts to one side. He pours himself a Scotch

Elizabeth returns

Roddy's got the car. That's why I can't find the car keys. He's taken the car without permission.
Colin (*returning to the sofa*) Oh God! I *said* give him driving lessons.
Elizabeth He's too young.
Colin He's legally old enough.
Elizabeth You know my views on that. All those teenagers killed every year. (*She starts to dial on the phone*)
Colin Surely it's better for him to be taught properly than going off with God-knows-who. You're not ringing the police?
Elizabeth Louise? ... Are you going to the cooking do tonight? ... You are? Could I beg a lift off you—ours has broken down ... Oh thanks. What time are you ... Good. Tell you what—give us a couple of rings when you're leaving and I'll meet you on the corner ... Thanks—that's a great help. 'Bye.
Colin I'll have a word with Roddy when he gets back.
Elizabeth *If* he gets back. (*She sits on the swivel chair*)
Colin Don't be silly. I really think he ought to have lessons.
Elizabeth We'll talk about it later. Have you applied for McIntosh's job yet?
Colin Not yet.
Elizabeth Applications close soon, don't they?
Colin (*lying back*) Plenty of time.
Elizabeth You don't sound too keen. I thought that was what you were waiting for—the chance to be a headmaster—that was your ambition.
Colin The only ambition I have left now is that one day I shall own a raincoat I'm not ashamed of.
Elizabeth Well, don't leave it too late.
Colin You sound like my father. "Too late—the saddest words in the English language—the saddest words in the English language." I don't know how

many times he said that to me. He used it as a goad to get me to work for exams.

Elizabeth Well, *don't* leave it too late.

The phone rings twice and stops. Elizabeth gets up to go

That's Louise! Don't forget to write to my mother to thank her for those underpants she sent for your birthday.

Colin Tonight I have all the reports to do.

Elizabeth And you will talk to Roddy, won't you.

Colin It won't do any good.

Elizabeth goes

Colin pulls his briefcase towards him. He gets out some reports and a pen. He stares at the first one

Martin Knox? Martin Knox?? (*He writes*) "Could do better." (*He reaches for the next one, pauses, then writes*) "Expresses himself clearly." Rude little sod.

Reg (*off*) Anybody home?

Colin In here.

Reg comes in

Reg Doing reports?

Colin Yes, Reg.

Reg Terrible business.

Colin Yes, Reg.

Reg Just put "Could do better".

Colin Yes, Reg.

Reg Have you got Stephen's there? Save me a trip to talk to his teachers.

Colin I don't think so.

Reg He's doing all right, isn't he?

Colin As far as I know. He's certainly keen on his writing. Doing good work on the school paper. Some of the kids want him to be editor next term.

Reg Do they? He never told me. (*He sits in the swivel chair*) What's the new woman like? Judy something.

Colin She's all right. Why?

Reg Somebody just mentioned her the other day. Split up from her husband or something.

Colin I believe so.

Reg You putting in for McIntosh's job?

Colin I don't know.

Reg It would be marvellous, running your own school. The ideas you could introduce—you could really get the place swinging. There's so much needs doing.

Colin You put in for the job, then.

Reg I'm primary. I wouldn't mind—even a primary school—but you've got to go back teaching first—I've been too long away. The whole system's upside down—if you're a really good teacher, they promote you out of the classroom. If you're a terrible teacher, they keep you there. It's a wonder kids get any education at all. No, the only way out of Teachers' College for me is to become an inspector.

Colin Become one, then.

Reg Me! An inspector! Actually I did apply once, but ... Ah, I'm far too outspoken for them.

Colin Well, you get no sympathy from me—I'm just as trapped as you are. Was there any particular reason you came round?

Reg Mm? (*Rising and wandering around*) Oh, just Isobel's cottage industries were driving me mad. If it's not the trundle of the spinning wheel or the slap of clay, it's the tap of tiny hammers on silver. Now she's into leather—though not in a way I might appreciate. Little clicks and snips—Christ, I'm expecting a bunch of elves to appear any moment. Got any Scotch?

Colin (*after a slight pause*) It's in the cupboard.

Reg Thanks. (*Pouring*) You want one? (*He drinks*)

Colin No, thanks.

Reg Bad for your figure? (*He pours another drink*)

Colin I'm trying to work.

Reg Well, you are putting it on a bit these days. (*Pause*) I'm having the most fantastic affair.

Colin Reg, I don't want to hear about it.

Reg (*sitting*) She's nineteen—a second-year. Fantastic looker—all the male students drool over her. In bed, she's incredible—she ...

Colin Reg, didn't you go through all this a couple of years ago?

Reg This is different. You know, I'd forgotten what it was like to be in love. We nip off to her place afternoons and ...

Colin Reg, I really don't want to know.

Reg You're just jealous.

Colin Yes I'm jealous. Jealous you've got that much energy apart from anything else. But I've got reports to do—I've got a son out there somewhere using the car as a drag racer—I've got an overcooked dinner waiting for me in the oven—I'm in no mood to listen to a catalogue of your coital positions.

Reg drains his glass and stands up to go

Reg The trouble with you is that life is passing you by—and you're only just realizing it.

Colin Yes, Reg. Anything you say, Reg.

Reg goes

The outer door bangs. Colin sits for a moment looking dejected. Then he stands and measures the size of his stomach in his hands. Definitely the makings of a paunch. He produces from his briefcase a small parcel which he unwraps to reveal a copy of 5BX. He skims through the pages and then reads. After a moment he begins to do the first of the exercises. He does two or three "knees-bends", then falls over, as the Lights fade and—

the CURTAIN *falls*

Scene 3

Judy's bed-sitter. An evening in May, a few days after Scene 2

Only a corner of the room is seen. There is a double bed, which makes it seem cramped. There is one chair. Some record covers can be seen and there is a pile of books on a bedside table

Judy and Colin enter. Judy is wearing coat which she takes off. Colin is wearing his raincoat

Colin I can only stay a minute.
Judy (*switching on pendant light*) But you can stay for coffee?

Judy exits to leave her coat in the hall

Colin Yes, thanks.
Judy (*off; calling*) Sit down . . . make yourself comfortable.
Colin Thanks. (*He sits down. Then gets up to take off his coat. He does not know where to put the wretched thing. Finally he rolls it up as small as possible and tucks it just under the chair*)

Judy sticks her head in

Judy Milk and sugar?
Colin Please.

Judy exits

Oh—no sugar. I'm giving it up. (*He goes to the books, chooses one, and moves away*)

Judy enters with two mugs of coffee and closes the door. She gives him one, then picks up a book

Judy I've just finished this one. He goes right round Europe and Asia by railway. It sounds marvellous. Paul Theroux—*The Great Railway Bazaar*. Have you read it?
Colin No. I've read some of his others. Good?
Judy Super. You'd like it. Borrow it, if you like.
Colin May I? Thanks, I will. (*He sits on the armchair*)

Judy takes off her shoes and tucks up her feet to sit on the bed

Judy Not much room. How the married couple who were here before managed I don't know. They had to leave because she was having a baby. "No pets or children allowed."
Colin It's—nice.
Judy No it's not. But it's mine. I feel like I did when I first left home. You know, that feeling of being able to do exactly what you want—and not making the bed first thing like your mother always told you.
Colin Yes.
Judy Some afternoons I come home from school and get straight into bed

and just read. Bliss! That's the trouble with kids—you never get a chance to read.

Colin How long have you been here?

Judy About two months. I moved in here straight away after I—after I left. Luckily that supply job at school turned up almost immediately.

Colin Why did—sorry. None of my business.

Judy "Why did I leave him?"

Colin Yes.

Judy (*after thinking for a moment*) Because every time I heard him arrive home my heart would sink.

A pause

Colin I see.

Judy Do you? Nobody else does. Robert was a model husband—good job, spent plenty of time with the kids—and with me. Never got drunk, always came home when he said he would. We never even rowed! But it was all so—calculated—so unspontaneous. He once left his business diary open by the phone and I read an entry in it for a week ahead "Buy Judy flowers". It wasn't a special occasion or anything—I'm sure he read in a marriage manual or somewhere that you should buy little surprise presents for your wife occasionally. Sure enough, on the day, he arrived home with flowers.

Colin Some women never get flowers.

Judy I know. That's what's so silly. He likes doing the right thing—he always wants to do good, but he's never quite sure how to go about it. That's why he joined the Rotary Club.

Colin There are worse things to join.

Judy I was so young when we got married. God, when I think of it now. He was always well-mannered and well-dressed. And we would obviously have a nice house and there would always be plenty of money. For the rest of my life. That all seemed so important at the time.

Colin How many children have you got?

Judy Three. Robert's got a Nannie looking after them.

Colin You must miss them.

Judy I do. Desperately at times. I'd rather not talk about it, if you don't mind. Are all parent-teacher meetings as bad as tonight?

Colin Bad?

Judy Long queues. Parents waiting for ages for a couple of minutes' talk. Some of the parents—I couldn't think who their children were. Very embarrassing.

Colin It happens to us all. And the parents you really want to see never turn up.

Judy It seemed so pointless.

Colin I sometimes think the whole secondary system's pointless—nothing that we can ever say or do's going to affect kids of that age—our only impact is a few marks either way in O levels.

Judy That sounds a bit despairing.

Colin How can we compete against colour TV, the breweries, and unskilled jobs with high wages. Compared to that lot, most kids can't see any point

in school at all. It all seems so futile—the kids from the good homes will
end up at the top—and the others at the bottom. School's just irrelevant.
Sorry—I always get this way after meeting the parents.

Judy Still, if you had a decent headmaster, that would help. Is McIntosh really
a pill—or is that just me?

Colin Oh, well ... He's retiring at the end of the term anyway.

Judy That's good. Who'll get his job?

Colin shrugs

Oh, you will! You're the assistant headmaster, you're almost bound to get
it.

Colin It doesn't always work out that way.

Judy It would be super if you did.

Colin I don't know. Often I can't seem to handle my own kids, let alone seven
hundred of someone else's.

Judy I wouldn't have thought Jane would be any trouble. We've always got
on very well at school whenever I've taught her.

Colin She's fine really—she has her moments. We're hoping she'll do well
enough in her A levels to go in for medicine—I think she'd make a good
doctor.

Judy And you've a son at the school, too, haven't you?

Colin Roddy. In the fifth. Basketball and cars at the moment—maybe other
passions as well but he keeps things to himself. And Caroline's almost five—
one of those unplanned events that took us all by surprise. Elizabeth still
resents her a bit, I think. I mean, she loves her, of course, but her arrival
messed up a lot of plans for her—she'd just been offered a good job.

Judy What did she do?

Colin Oh, secretary. She's been looking round for a part-time job for when
Caroline starts school, but there's not much doing at present. It'll do her
good to get back to work—she's stagnated a bit—inevitably I suppose, not
that she'd admit it—sorry, I'm talking far too much. Don't seem to get much
chance to talk these days.

Judy It's nice to have someone around here who only wants to talk. Men
assume as soon as your marriage packs up you're automatically available
sexually. The number of married men who call because they "just happen"
to be passing by, and they "just happen" to have a bottle of gin with them.
They've all got *The Joy of Sex* locked in their office drawer and are dying
to try it out. Preferably all in one evening. So—it's nice to be able to sit
here not waiting for the first lunge.

Colin I'm not really the lunging type.

Judy I didn't think you were. Have you ever ... I'm sorry—now it's my turn
to be personal.

Colin Go on.

Judy I was going to ask if you'd ever had an affair with another woman.

Colin No! I'd be far too frightened.

Judy Frightened! What on earth is there to be frightened of?

Colin Getting the woman pregnant or getting VD. Or both. Having my tes-
ticles shot off by an enraged husband; being jeered at in the playground

by pupils in the know. Elizabeth finding out and leaving with the children. Elizabeth finding out and leaving with*out* the children. Any known fear or combination of fears I've thought about them. I just don't think it would be worth it—as it is I get post-coital depression almost before I've finished, so if I added guilt on top of that!

Judy You are a worrier, aren't you. I've watched you at school in your funny old jacket—

Colin Is it?

Judy —worrying about timetables and duty rosters and whether the supply teacher's turned up and what the boys are up to with the girls.

Colin That's the job. General dog's body. Anyway—I must go. (*He rises*)

Judy (*rising*) Thanks for dropping me off.

Colin Pleasure.

Judy Call again.

Colin For a talk?

Judy For a talk.

As they make for the door she picks up the book

Judy Here—do take it.

Colin Thanks. (*He takes the book*)

Judy And don't worry.

Judy sees him out. The raincoat is still under the chair. The Lights fade, as—

the CURTAIN falls

<h1 style="text-align:center;">SCENE 4</h1>

The dinner party continued

They have just finished a fondue. *Only Reg and Colin are still fishing for bits. The phone is off the hook. Judy is out of the room*

Elizabeth Robert—do have some more.

Robert No—that was lovely.

Isobel Yes it was.

Reg I always think a *fondue* is symbolic of life, don't you? Everyone jabbing away for the best bits.

Isobel And him making sure he gets them.

Colin, after careful manoeuvring, produces his fork. It is empty

Reg Ah! (*He produces his fork—he has caught a piece. He eats it and peers in again*) That seems to be it.

Colin You should know.

Judy enters from the hall

Robert Everything all right?

Elizabeth replaces the telephone on its cradle

Judy Tim woke up crying evidently—was a bit upset. I talked to him on the phone and he seemed to settle down.

Robert You don't think we should go home?

Judy No—I told her to ring again if he didn't go back to sleep. He'll be all right.

Isobel Do you know—I've just been trying to remember—the last time I had *fondue* must have been in Switzerland. *Après ski*, and all that.

Elizabeth Oh I loved Switzerland. I once had three months there. As a secretary—my firm sent me out.

Isobel You lucky thing—I never knew that.

Elizabeth Mm.

Isobel But the place I'm determined to go back to—Florence.

Elizabeth collects the plates, Isobel helping her, and puts them on a tray

Elizabeth Oh yes!

Reg Oh God, we're not off on our travel reminiscences are we. Nine days here one year, a fortnight somewhere else the next. Rabbiting on about the Spanish Steps, and having one's undies stolen in Greek camping grounds. Judy, are you another who's done the Grand Tour on the instalment plan?

Judy Costa Brava, eight days. It was where I met Robert actually.

Reg Ohhhhhh! Honestly, you women, you make me sick. You all rushed round, having holidays all the time, went off to New York and places to be temps, asked out everywhere, having a whale of a time, while us men were supposed to keep our noses to the grindstone and get qualified.

Isobel I *worked* to get him through his final year!

Elizabeth And I had a very big bottom drawer. You've never resented my travelling have you?

Colin Yes. I did!

Isobel opens the kitchen door

Elizabeth You never said anything. Thank you.

Elizabeth exits with the tray

Isobel He pretends to sneer at travel, but he's always rushing home and saying "Let's go and live in Mexico for a couple of years", or suggesting we go round the world by Land Rover. It's just as well I'm there to bring him down to earth. (*She sits at the table again*)

Reg Very hard to love someone who's always bringing you down to earth.

A slight pause while this sinks in

Robert We haven't done much travelling, but we are going on a cruise to the Greek Islands next month.

Reg Super! I am glad!

Isobel Take no notice of him Robert. He's in a foul mood—some little nineteen-year-old's just thrown him over. Every eighteen months or so, he rushes off with some first year—he thinks it's part of the job.

Reg It is.
Colin (*rising with a bottle of white wine*) My dear fellow, I am sorry. You must have some more drink.
Reg What is it this time? A National Coal Board burgundy or a British Leyland sauterne?
Colin (*pouring*) Well, whatever it is, I know you won't say no. Isobel?
Isobel No more for me—I already feel quite a flush.
Colin Robert? (*He pours red wine for Robert*)
Robert I should've bought some of those wines. I thought at the time they were a good buy, but with prices the way they are now...
Reg Now come on, Colin, I'm waiting to hear what you're going to do with the school. Get kids literally to pull their socks up ... or what?
Colin No, no, no. (*He sits*)
Reg Judy! You've seen the school with new eyes comparatively recently—and now you're leaving you can give a disinterested opinion—what do you think needs doing to the place?

Elizabeth enters with an empty tray

Colin Painting for a start.
Judy I'm not sure ... there's a terrible restlessness about the place—
Elizabeth Children are restless these days. (*During the following she collects empty dishes and bottles on to her tray*)
Judy I meant among the staff. You know—everyone grabbing the *Times Educational Supplement* as soon as it arrives to look for another position.
Isobel When we were at school, the teachers stayed for *years*!
Judy I'm sure it can't be good for pupils—the turnover of staff. But that's only part of it—things like forty-minute periods. Television's blamed for reducing people's concentration span—but it's absurd to chop up a day into chunks of forty minutes! I don't know—there's an aura of impermanence—about everything.
Colin That's because nothing *is* permanent. Not long ago it was Social Studies that had to be taught in a completely different way—now it's English. You have to edit films and splice tapes to be able to teach English. I find it harder and harder to keep up.
Reg The system's built upside down! Here's old Colin, putting it on round the middle, his opinions hardening almost as fast as his arteries, and what happens—he gets put in a position where he's expected to be in the vanguard of change.
Colin I can feel the word "reactionary" settling over me like a cloud. I'll get more and more skilful at finding reasons why things shouldn't be done.
Judy No, you won't.
Colin At least Roddy's shown no sign of wanting to go in for teaching.
Isobel Yes, what does Roddy want to do?
Elizabeth Well, Jane wants to be a doctor. Did I tell you she'd decided to go in for medicine?
Isoobel Yes.
Elizabeth But Roddy hasn't said what he wants to be.
Colin (*opening the kitchen door*) Yes he has—he wants to run his own garage.

Elizabeth Yes, isn't it silly?

Elizabeth exits with the tray

Isobel I always say it doesn't matter what you want to be. You can be a dustman if you like as long as you're a *good* dustman.
Colin I certainly wouldn't let Roddy be a dustman.
Judy Wouldn't you?
Colin Mainly because I'm frightened of them. I don't know why it is, but whenever I hear them coming up the path I always want to hide.
Reg It's guilt that we haven't got a manual job.
Colin You're probably right. Elizabeth's father still regards me as not doing a man's job because I teach. You know—if you don't get your hands dirty doing it, it's obviously a job for softies. Staying there's like a permanent commercial for a hand-cleanser; he's always getting me to help him change the oil in the car, or get all the leaves out of the spouting. Just the same with women—Elizabeth's mother's job is to make sure the men of the family are clothed and fed. Mind you—it works very well. (*He sits*)

Elizabeth enters

Reg That won't wash with kids these days. At least they've seen through all that sex rôle crap.

Elizabeth collects the salad bowl and servers

Elizabeth I think that's such a pity. I don't think there was anything ever wrong with treating a woman as a lady. Nowadays they have no idea of manners. The other day I had to go to town on the bus because the car was in the garage—and it was full of schoolchildren. And do you know, not one of them offered me their seat!

Elizabeth exits to the kitchen

Isobel I know!
Reg You two must join the real world some time.
Robert I think one reason things have changed for the worse is that not enough school pupils play team sport. You learn an awful lot from playing a team sport. I know I did.
Colin I'm not so sure. I was reffing a school soccer match last term and Mike Gillespie, playing at back, suddenly smashes the ball past his own goalkeeper into the net. I said "What did you do that for?" and he said, "Just wanted to see what it was like to score a goal, man!"
Robert I would have sent him off the field.
Colin He wouldn't've gone.
Robert Then abandon the game.
Colin There would've been a flurry of V-signs at my departing back and they'd've carried on without me.
Reg Yes, hooray for the Mike Gillespies, I say. I mean, forgive me old man, but it really is a load of twaddle to say team sports develop the character and all that—look at the sorts of unpleasantness that occur even in so-called friendly matches.

Robert Yes, but team sports teach you to learn to take it—to take hard knocks. And to accept decisions—say in cricket—accept a decision from the umpire that you disagree with.

Reg What use is all that! What hard knocks do you have to take in your job? Don't tell me there's someone who tries to knee you in the groin every time you reach for the calculator. And as for accepting decisions when they go against you! Your whole job is based on *not* accepting them! You're fighting the Inland Revenue's decisions every day.

Robert No, that's not quite...

Reg And then people like you tell kids that if they trudge back to the pavilion manfully when they know bloody well they weren't out, that this will stand them in good stead all their life. Do me a bloody favour!

Robert Yes, but it's...

Reg Kids can see through all that. When we try and tell them it doesn't matter if you lose, they *know* we're talking bull. They know enough about life to realize winning's everything now. And that's typical of the sort of stuff we feed them—no wonder they disbelieve ninety per cent of everything else we say.

During the above speech Elizabeth returns to collect the fondue *and catches the drift of the conversation*

Elizabeth I didn't mind losing at tennis.

Elizabeth exits to the kitchen

Colin She does now.

Pause

Isobel I wish Stephen hadn't believed some of the things he was told in our house.

Pause. Reg rises and moves away

Reg Will somebody tell her to shut up about that.

The Lights fade, as—

the CURTAIN *falls*

SCENE 5

Elizabeth's and Colin's bedroom. June 8th

Elizabeth is in bed, putting cream on her face and reading a magazine

Elizabeth (*calling*) Is the cat out?
Colin (*off*) Yes!

Pause

(*Off*) Where are the tissues?

Elizabeth There's a new box on the fridge.

Colin comes in wearing pyjamas. He has a cold. He is carrying a box of tissues which he has just opened. He does a double-take when he sees Elizabeth

Colin Oh. Oh!

Elizabeth What?

Colin Nothing. (*He picks up his 5BX book and begins doing his Canadian Air Force exercises, which irritates Elizabeth*)

Elizabeth Aren't you going for a run tonight?

Colin No. (*He is puffing quite a bit*)

Elizabeth You don't seem much fitter for it.

Colin Wad?

Elizabeth For the running you've done at night.

Colin It's by cold! (*He stops*) Oh, I can't do any bore!*

Colin gets into bed, reaches for "The Great Railway Bazaar" and finds his place. A silence except for his sniffing and nose-blowing all of which annoy Elizabeth

Elizabeth You'll either have to find your raincoat or buy a new one.

Colin I'm sure it's at school.

Elizabeth Who's in charge of lost property?

Colin I am. (*He blows his nose again*)

Elizabeth That's how you got the cold in the first place—going out in the rain without—

Colin You told me.

Pause

Elizabeth I took Caroline to enrol her at school today.

Colin Good.

Elizabeth The teacher seemed very nice.

Colin Good.

Pause

Elizabeth (*showing him the magazine*) Those blinds would look nice in our kitchen.

Colin (*glancing at them*) Mm.

Elizabeth And I thought those shutters would make a big difference to the front of the house.

Colin Who would shut them?

Elizabeth They don't shut—they're not meant to shut.

Colin Ah!

Elizabeth reads for a moment more then puts the magazine away and settles down

Elizabeth Have you put in for the job?

Colin Not yet.

Elizabeth Well, you haven't much time. (*She puts out her bedside lamp*)

Colin I know. I know.

* From now on, Colin's speeches are printed normally; the actor should devise his own "cold" pronunciation.

He carries on reading. She drifts off to sleep, unnoticed by him. He finishes a page, carefully marks the place. He then blows vigorously and finally clears both nostrils with a nasal spray. This done he turns to Elizabeth with an expectant smile and is furious to find her asleep

Oh for heavens' sake!
Elizabeth Wha—wha...?
Colin You're not asleep!
Elizabeth What is it? What's happened?
Colin If I come to bed at the same time as you, you know why!
Elizabeth Colin, I'm tired out! I want to go to sleep.
Colin It's not as if I do this very often. Either you're having your period fourteen days out of twenty-eight, or your parents are within a fifty mile radius and might hear—or there's an "R" in the month—or *something*!
Elizabeth Rubbish.
Colin I feel I should book you thirty-five days in advance like one of those cheap air fares. And on the rare occasions I do like to enjoy my conjugal rights you never exactly welcome any overtures I make.
Elizabeth What on earth is there to welcome!! You come in here, prance about with the crutch out of your pyjamas, get into bed sweating and puffing and sniffing—you read your ten pages of your wretched book—and *then*, twenty seconds later, I'm supposed to be shouting and moaning in ecstasy.
Colin All I ask is that occasionally you make an effort.
Elizabeth All I ask is that you understand that when I get to bed I'm tired out. Caroline is a very demanding child—to say nothing of seeing you're all decently fed and clothed. And trying to keep the house clean. And the garden!
Colin I know all that, I know all that.
Elizabeth So that by the time I do get to bed all I want to do is go to sleep!
Colin I know all that. All I'm saying is just for once, just once in a while, come to bed not looking like your mother, actually come to bed looking nice and with some scent on—and make the effort. It's not much to ask.
Elizabeth All right then, I'll make an effort. Come on then.
Colin What?
Elizabeth Come *on*.
Colin What sort of invitation is that?
Elizabeth Do you want to, or don't you?
Colin Let's forget the whole thing, shall we?
Elizabeth Right. Fine. Suits me. Just don't say I wasn't willing. (*She goes back to sleep*)

Colin goes back to his book and reads a bit more, but then closes the book. He then snuggles up to Elizabeth again

Colin Elizabeth—I've changed my mind.

But she is asleep for good this time. Colin lies back and stares at the ceiling. The Lights fade, as—

the CURTAIN *falls*

SCENE 6

Judy's bed-sitter. A few days after Scene 5

Colin is still lying in bed, though this time without pyjamas on, staring at the ceiling. Judy's back can be seen in the doorway. She is wearing a dressing-gown and is talking on the telephone

Judy Robert—I've said when I'll be there ... Yes—exactly the same time as usual. I've never let them down yet—*don't* go into all that ... (*Firmly*) I'll see you Sunday ... Yes! 'Bye. (*She rings off and comes in*) That was Robert—as you probably gathered.
Colin Yes. For a horrible moment, I thought he must know about...
Judy No! Tim's got his rash again—he wanted to know where I keep the ointment. And to confirm when I'd be seeing the kids again—it's his way of nagging—I see them the same time every week.
Colin It was almost as if he sensed something.
Judy He certainly mistimed things. (*She lies on the bed*) Next time, I'll take the phone off the hook—if you want there to be a next time.
Colin Yes.
Judy Well ...? Do you want to carry on where we left off? Or ...?
Colin Perhaps—leave it—tonight.
Judy Yes.
Colin I can't stay.
Judy I quite understand.
Colin Sorry.
Judy Quite all right. Tell me, did you plan tonight—like this?
Colin No, I just thought I'd drop in for a chat...
Judy For another chat.
Colin Another chat—I don't know what came over me.
Judy I think it's called "lust".
Colin I'm sorry.
Judy Nothing to be sorry about. I'm not. I wasn't exactly stopping you, was I?
Colin No, but...

She kisses him

Judy You really are nice.
Colin That's as bad as saying "He means well".
Judy No it's not. You're nice to people at school—kids as well as adults. That's increasingly rare these days—it's the word that's been debased, not the quality.
Colin Mm.
Judy You mustn't run yourself down.
Colin Oh well...
Judy And I hear you applied for the headmaster's job—that's super.
Colin Against my better judgment.
Judy Why did you apply, then?

Colin Because Elizabeth nagged me. Because you're *trained* to want to be a headmaster. Because assistant head's a lousy job. Because if you're assistant head too long people think you're a failure. I don't know. "Nice"! Am I being nice to Elizabeth right now?

Judy Look—if you want to go to bed with me—fine. If you want to discuss ethics, go somewhere else.

Pause

Do I gather things between you and Elizabeth aren't too good?

Colin No! Things are fine—you know, average. I mean we don't talk much—apart from who's got the car keys—things like that—we never get time to talk. Anyway, we know each other's opinions on everything by now.

Judy Do you still love her?

Colin Compared to what? Yes—I suppose so. Affection flares up every now and then—but it's mainly habit. You must know what it's like.

Judy Yes.

Colin Does Robert ring you a lot?

Judy Quite a bit.

Colin He wants you to go back, I suppose?

Judy Mmm. Feeling sorry for him isn't a good enough reason, is it—to go back to him?

Colin I wouldn't think so.

Judy I don't think so either. Going back—it would almost be like going back to prison. The kids are jailers—you can't leave the house without them, you can't do anything without at least one pair of eyes watching. You sit down for a moment and you have to get up; you eat your meals on the run; any phone call lasts only until a fight breaks out. You can't even go to the lavatory in peace! I just—I just don't think I can face it all again. Here—I'm a new person—I can read, I can listen to music, I can lie on the bed and think—I really am a new person. I can't go back now.

Colin What will you...?

Judy I'm going to go abroad.

Colin Where?

Judy Anywhere. Europe—Asia. Just take off. Do what Theroux did in the book. Or John Hillaby—walk. It doesn't much matter. Just travelling ... for as long as I possibly can.

Colin Yes. I wish I'd done all that. All my mates at college, they used to hitch-hike all over the place—Istanbul, North Africa. All I did was youth hostelling in bloody Wales. I'll never do it now, will I. All that. It's too late. (*Looking at his watch*) Elizabeth'll wonder where I've got to. Oh! My raincoat—don't let me forget it this time.

Judy I took it to school. I meant to give it to you today.

Colin Hell.

Judy Sorry.

Colin Listen—about tonight—it can't lead to anything, I mean, I've no intention of leaving Elizabeth—I ...

Judy I know, I know.

Colin I just thought I should make it clear.

Judy I understand all that.
Colin I feel bad enough about being a rat to Elizab—
Judy Almost a rat.
Colin Almost a rat—I don't want to end up being a rat to you as well.
Judy Go home. Forget your rodent problem, and go home to your wife and
family.

Judy kisses him, as the Lights fade, and—

the CURTAIN *falls*

SCENE 7

The dinner party continued

*The three men are alone—in relaxed silence. Reg is sitting in the swivel chair,
Colin and Robert at the table. Robert drinks, then puts his glass down, takes
his cigarettes from his pocket and offers them to Reg, who shakes his head.
He offers them to Colin*

Colin No thanks—I've given it up.
Robert Lucky man. How did you do it?
Colin Fear was a great incentive. Fear of cancer.

Robert sits again

Reg You've got to die of something.
Colin Not only that, but coughing my lungs up every morning began to lose
its appeal.
Reg You won't get cancer—you're more coronary material.
Colin Don't think I haven't thought of that. At the moment, I'm trying to
give up sugar—you know—white sugar, white death.
Robert What about butter?
Colin Oh yes, that was the first thing to go. Margarine on everything. Now
I'm doing jogging and the Canadian Air Force exercises.
Reg They'll never accept you in the Canadian Air Force at your age!
Robert Hm—I see I'll have to get cracking. I've always found it very hard
to relax—I find I'm very tense at work. That's a bad sign, for one.
Reg Well I wouldn't take Colin's jogging too seriously—he only uses it to—
oh never mind.
Colin It's silly, isn't it—how we worry about all this. I used to think that as
you grew older—the more you'd had of your allotted lifespan and the less
you had to lose—you'd be less and less fearful. Instead, I've grown increasingly frightened of all sorts of things. I'll give you a for instance. You know
those huge cranes on building sites. And they have those whacking great
paving stone things to counterbalance them—four or five bolted together.
Well I'm convinced that one day they're going to hurtle down right when
I'm walking underneath. I find myself crossing over the road to avoid going
anywhere near them. The latest thing I've noticed is that I'm getting very

twitchy when someone else is driving the car—I'm developing into the
classic backseat driver.

Robert With me it's memory. I used to be able to remember everything—
dates, appointments, titles of films I saw years ago—now I have to write
everything down. I have to have a business diary for everything. What about
you? You must find the same sort of thing?

Reg No.

Colin There must be something.

Reg Nothing.

Colin It all seems so unfair, somehow. You knew it was all going to happen,
but not quite so soon. Do you know I sometimes catch myself thinking—
even now—thinking of myself as a young man with promise.

Robert And now you're virtually at the top of your profession.

Colin Mm. And doubtless retirement will take me by surprise.

Robert Absent-mindedness is another thing. The other day I was taking out
the milk bottles on the way out—and I found myself halfway down the street
and they were still in my hand.

The three women enter from the kitchen

Colin and Robert rise

Judy Elizabeth's just been showing us her new blinds.

Robert Are they nice?

Judy Very.

They all sit around the table

Robert Well, you can have some if you want.

Judy (*annoyed*) No, I didn't mean that.

Elizabeth Roddy's back from basketball. They won.

Colin Good.

Elizabeth And the car's all right.

Isobel And Judy's just been telling us about your cruise to the Greek Islands
next month. It sounds wonderful. What a lovely idea to celebrate your ...
I mean, if I went back to Reg after we'd—you know, after ... *He* certainly
wouldn't ...

Robert (*rescuing her*) We were lucky. Got a cancellation. Most cruises—
booked out.

Elizabeth I know! That's what I can't understand when they say there's no
money about.

Reg I don't think you'd find many of the unemployed in the queue for
P. & O. cancellations.

Elizabeth Oh well, of course I wouldn't know about that.

Reg Living on the dole. Twenty-five pounds a week. Do me a favour.

Colin I wouldn't like to manage on that, I must admit.

Elizabeth We could manage—easily. Perhaps we'd have to scrimp and save
a bit, but that's just what these people aren't prepared to do. They complain
about how difficult it is, but they've all got cars and colour television and
go to the pub all the time. We could manage, Colin.

Reg Yes, but you've got everything. You've got your house and car and deep freeze and wall-to-wall carpet in the lavatory. Imagine if you were starting off to get all those things and having to pay thirty to forty pounds a week rent.

Judy You're quite right.

Reg And as for an Englishman's home is his castle—how many people can even contemplate buying a house these days.

Elizabeth But there are council houses. Subsidized by the rate-payers. And look how people treat them—some of them are left in a terrible mess. I'm sorry but I can't feel sorry for these people. For years Colin was earning less than most unskilled workers. Look at first-year doctors in hospitals— the porters and cleaners earn more than they do. It's about time we had our turn.

Reg My God, Elizabeth, your hair's turning prematurely blue.

Elizabeth And as for the unemployed, well—all right. But almost invariably they were the lot that mucked about at school, making life hell for the teachers, and wasting everybody's time and the tax-payers' money. You don't find people with A levels out of work.

Colin What worries me is that for all the great pieces of social engineering, the nineteen forty-four Education Act, the comprehensives, all that—the end result is still the same: the kids from the good homes end up on top, and the ones from the bad homes stay at the bottom.

Judy Yes but what do you do about it? Don't you feel helpless?

Colin Yes.

Reg At one time you used to feel that who you voted for made a difference. Now it's just a waste of time.

Colin It certainly is for me. I only go along to the polls to wipe out Elizabeth's vote for the Conservatives. And she only votes for the local chap because she thinks he's such a nice man.

Elizabeth Well, he is. He's got nice manners and I think that's important. Most of the Labour people are so—coarse. And in any case I'm a great admirer of Margaret Thatcher.

Reg Yes, I know, I've seen your cupboards. Jammed full with tinned goods. Well—I still vote for the coarse lot, heaven help me. I mean, God knows they have their faults, but at least they *aim* to bring about a measure of fairness and equality, however lamentably far they fall short of their target. The Conservatives don't stand for anything; they're only united by a common bond to keep out Labour at all costs.

Judy What worries me is whatever one side does, the other tries to undo as soon as it gets into power. They just meet head-on all the time. What is it called—"the politics of confrontation"?

Isobel It's all so wasteful.

Colin It's hopeless—hopeless.

Robert I think you're all wrong. Things have taken a turn for the better. For years and years, people have assumed that if things go wrong, the Government will come to their aid. It's killed initiative and the development of new ideas—there's no incentive for them. Now I think people are realizing that you can't always rely on the State for a handout—and the way out of the mess is to knuckle down to a bit of hard work.

Reg Roll up our sleeves, man the lathes, dig for victory. A fair day's work for a fair day's pay.

Robert Yes, except as soon as a man tries to do a fair day's work the unions won't allow him to. They're out to wreck the economy, as we all know.

Reg That is so middle-class it makes my flesh crawl.

Robert (*suddenly furious*) Why is "middle-class" now a term of abuse? Every one of us in this room is middle-class—all that means is that we were brought up to work hard to get a decent sort of job and try and lead reasonable sort of lives. Dammit, I *did* work hard—and still do—and I do try to lead a decent life—and blowed if I'm going to be made to feel ashamed of it.

Elizabeth Hear hear!

Reg Oh Lord!

Isobel It's the middle classes that keep this country going. They're the ones on the school committees, the ones who keep most of the good causes in voluntary workers. And if it was not for the middle-classes we'd have next to no culture to speak of.

Elizabeth Anyway Reg, you must agree that with all England's faults, you wouldn't want to live anywhere else. America for instance.

Reg Oh Elizabeth! You must believe everything *The Daily Telegraph* tells you! Why this absurd prejudice against America? I'd *love* to live in America, or West Germany or Switzerland or a dozen other places you care to name. You must think Britain is some last bastion of decency, fair play and all that. That somehow we're the moral superiors of the rest of the world, all of us still regular chaps, wouldn't let a fellow down, don't you know. Decency is in our genetic code. Whereas in fact we're as nasty, prejudiced, violent, alcohol-addicted, and hypocritical as the rest of the world.

A silence

Colin I'll drink to that. (*He drinks*)

Elizabeth I'll go to get the dessert.

Elizabeth goes to the kitchen. Judy gets up and goes out to the hall

Colin Anyhow, Reg—what are you going to do with your holidays?

Isobel He's solving the world's problems by going scuba diving in the Mediterranean.

Robert Lucky man.

Isobel Not taking me, of course. Says we can't afford it.

Robert It's an expensive sport.

Colin What isn't these days. Books! The school's book allowance buys exactly half what it did three years ago. I don't know what's going to happen in the future.

Judy enters

Judy Excuse me—did you know your daughter seems to be crying in her room?

Colin Oh thanks. (*Rising*) Probably Teddy-bear's developed bubonic plague.

Judy No—your other daughter—Jane.

Colin Oh.

Colin goes out to the hall. Elizabeth comes in with the dessert—in long glasses

Isobel Oh, this looks lovely.

Judy Mm, it does.

Elizabeth Well, the proof of the pudding's in the eating. Oh—it applies, doesn't it. (*She sits*)

Isobel It's funny how we take all these old sayings for granted.

Reg Life is one long process of verifying proverbs.

Judy Who said that?

Reg I did. Made it up myself. (*Rising*) Copyright of course—may only be used with express permission of the author.

Colin comes in

Judy Was everything all right?

Colin Not really.

Elizabeth What's the matter?

Judy Jane was crying in her room.

Elizabeth Probably some boy hasn't asked her to a dance. Crying at her age.

Colin I'm afraid it's a bit more than that.

Elizabeth What's...?

Colin She rather thinks she's pregnant.

Elizabeth Oh no!!

Colin To Stephen.

Isobel Oh no. (*She rises*) Oh no. We knew he'd got some girl—he told us tonight—but he wouldn't tell us who.

Reg I thought it was the journalist in him refusing to reveal his source.

Elizabeth She can't be! Surely not. (*She gets up to go to see her*)

Colin No. She said she wanted to see Judy. Would you mind?

Judy (*surprised*) No—(*rising*)—if it'll be of any help, sure.

Judy goes out to the hall

A silence. No-one knows what to say

Reg Well, since we're going to share the same grandchild, shall we be Granny and Gramps, and you Grandma and Grandpa, or would you prefer to be Grandad and ... The bloody little fools. (*He sits*)

The Lights fade, as—

the CURTAIN *falls*

SCENE 8

The sitting-room. June 29th

Colin is sitting in the swivel chair, slippers on, reading part of the paper. His shoes are by the chair, as is his briefcase. Elizabeth has the rest of the evening paper spread out on the floor in bits where she is reading it. They each have a cup of coffee

Elizabeth No jobs.
Colin Never mind—one'll turn up.

They exchange sheets. The telephone rings. Elizabeth answers it

Elizabeth (*on the phone*) Hallo ... Yes ... I see. Who is it speaking please?
... Just a minute. (*She goes to the door and calls*) Jane! Phone for you. (*She
puts the phone back on the hook*)

*Suddenly rock music blares from off stage. Colin gets up, but not angrily, and
goes to the door. We see, rather than hear, him shout "Turn it down". He realizes
he can't be heard and goes off. A moment later the music can be heard only
faintly with the door open, and not at all when he comes back in and shuts the
door. He sits down again*

Colin One of Roddy's mates has just bought a new amplifier. Trying it out
on our speakers. You know how I used to picture our family life when the
kids got this age? All of us sitting round of an evening listening to Haydn
quartets. Summers roaming the downs quoting Pope and Dryden. Enjoying
fine wines over dinners where sparkling conversation and witty repartee
reigned. And look how it turned out—they much prefer listening to *Blondie*
and eating *Big Macs*.
Elizabeth They should be doing their homework, not listening to rock music.
Colin They're listening to rock music *and* doing their homework.
Elizabeth I wasn't allowed to listen to the radio until I'd done all my work.
Colin For kids nowadays, there's nothing so distracting as silence.

Pause, as they continue reading the paper

Elizabeth Oh I ordered the blinds for the kitchen—I hope you don't mind.
Colin Of course not.
Elizabeth They'll be here next week.
Colin Good. Oh, I bought you a little present. (*He rummages in his briefcase
and produces small parcel*) Or, to be more accurate—I bought *us* a present.

Elizabeth unwraps the parcel—a box of chocolates

Elizabeth Oh nice. Thanks. (*She takes one and hands him the box*)
Colin I say, shall we have a liqueur?
Elizabeth Er ...
Colin It would be rather nice. I thought a bit later on I'd get our old record
player in here and we could listen to some Mozart.
Elizabeth All right, then.

He gets up and goes to the cupboard to pour two liqueurs

   I phoned Judy today.
Colin (*halting*) Why? What about?
Elizabeth To ask her for dinner.
Colin Here?
Elizabeth Yes. When we met at the staff social I said we must have her up.
Colin What did she say?
Elizabeth She couldn't manage the first two dates I suggested, but she can
make it Friday fortnight.

Colin That's the last day of term!
Elizabeth Oh. Is it?
Colin Yes.
Elizabeth Well, I can't change it now, I've asked Reg and Isobel.
Colin Oh no! Why?
Elizabeth We owe them a dinner. Two—if you count the drinks they had back
  in April. And I've asked the Hendersons and they're going to ring back.
Colin The Hendersons! We don't even like them! (*He puts Elizabeth's liqueur
  on the coffee-table*)
Elizabeth But we owe them an invitation.
Colin No we don't—it was Reg dragged us along uninvited to that party if
  you remember. We only went because you wanted to see inside their house.
Elizabeth Well, I've asked them now.

*Colin sits and tries to continue to read the paper, but the evening is ruined for
him now*

Colin Reg won't want to come on the last day of term.
Elizabeth It's all settled now.
Colin Nor will Judy for that matter.

Pause

  Bloody hell. (*He throws his paper on the floor*)

Pause

Elizabeth When do you hear about the job?
Colin I don't know.
Elizabeth Sorry.
Colin Don't keep asking, that's all.
Elizabeth Sorry.
Colin I don't particularly want the damn job anyway. Sick of the bloody place.
Elizabeth Is anything wrong at school?
Colin No.
Elizabeth *Something* must be ...
Colin No. Nothing. Wrightson's just had a nervous breakdown, keeping up
  our average of one-and-a-half per term; it's rained the last five sports days;
  the art room has had vandals in; seventy-four per cent of the pupils are
  waiting only for their sixteenth birthday. No—nothing's wrong—everything's exactly as bloody normal.
Elizabeth Sorry.
Colin (*rising*) Every day I have to turn up at that collection of ill-designed
  totally unaesthetic buildings, and worry about book grants and uniforms
  and lost property and drug problems and whether anyone's wanking in the
  toilets and everyone takes it for granted that all that's normal and it just
  pisses me off Elizabeth when I think of you sitting round all day doing nothing but read the fucking *House and Garden*!
Elizabeth Colin!
Colin Correction. I forgot—you also swap recipes and have coffee mornings.
Elizabeth You stay at home all day and see how you'd like it.

Colin I'd love it! I'd give my eye-teeth for the chance.
Elizabeth I've been trying to get a job—you know that!
Colin Trying!
Elizabeth That last job I went for—there were sixty-four applicants—most of them from women with degrees.
Colin What a pity you only got one A level!
Elizabeth That's not a very nice thing to say.

Short silence

Colin No. Sorry.
Elizabeth Is anything wrong?
Colin Nothing, nothing. No one thing—I can't explain.

Slight pause

Elizabeth You used to like teaching. (*She rises*)
Colin Did I?
Elizabeth I always thought you did.
Colin Maybe.
Elizabeth I can remember when we were first married you were full of the things you planned to do.
Colin Was I? Such as what?
Elizabeth Oh I can't remember exactly. New ways of teaching, of getting the kids more involved in planning their work—you used to come home really excited.
Colin That must have been before the inspectors came.
Elizabeth Do you remember that flat we were in then? With the bath that took half an hour to fill?
Colin Vaguely.
Elizabeth And you got so annoyed with it one night you banged the pipe with a hammer so hard that it came apart—we had water everywhere.
Colin Oh that's right! I had to get the plumber in.
Elizabeth It was a nice flat.
Colin It's not there, now. Pulled down. (*He puts his arm round her*) I'm sorry I was angry just now. (*He kisses her*)
Elizabeth That's all right. We used to go for walks.
Colin That's right.
Elizabeth You used to point out all the stars—you knew so many. It was lovely.

He remembers for a moment

Colin Let's go for a walk now.
Elizabeth Now?
Colin It's a beautiful night—it really is. It's a moon you could read by. We could go up the hill and look at the view. Come on.
Elizabeth Oh …
Colin Come on. You'll enjoy it.
Elizabeth I don't really feel like it.
Colin It wouldn't be for long.

Elizabeth I'd rather leave it. If you don't mind.
Colin Forget it. I'll go by myself. (*He sits and puts his slippers on, very angry with her*)
Elizabeth Perhaps tomorrow.
Colin Forget it.
Elizabeth I'd *like* to come—but it's a bit late—another time. (*She sits in the swivel chair*)

Colin exits without a word

The front door slams. There is a pause, then the telephone rings

Hallo? ... Who? ... Oh, Margaret *Henderson*! I'm sorry, for a moment, I was thinking of another Margaret ... You can't make that Friday ... Oh, what a pity ... Yes, I quite understand. Some other time, then ... Yes. 'Bye. (*She puts down the phone, sits on the sofa, helps herself to a chocolate, picks up "House and Garden" and begins looking through it*)

The Lights fade, as—

the CURTAIN *falls*

SCENE 9

Judy's bed-sitter. Early July, a few days after Scene 8

Colin and Judy are in bed. Judy is in a dressing-gown. The lighting is subdued and they are listening to music—the last bars of Janet Baker singing the Angel's Farewell from Elgar's "Dream of Gerontius". The music dies away and there is a silence as they are both absorbed in the music

Judy Want to hear some more?
Colin Better not.

Judy gets out of bed and turns off the record player

What's all this about you coming to dinner next week?
Judy Oh I'm sorry—I knew you wouldn't want me to come, but I ran out of excuses. Your wife is very persistent. (*She switches on the bedside lamp*)
Colin I know. Of course I want you to come—I'll just feel a bit awkward.
Judy As it turns out I may not be able to make it anyway.
Colin Oh?
Judy Tell you later.
Colin While you're up.
Judy Yes.
Colin Rummage among my clothes and see what you can find.

She looks in his clothes by the chair and finds a small package

Judy What's this?
Colin Present.

Judy What for?
Colin Our two months' anniversary. And a celebration.
Judy Celebration?
Colin I got the job—I heard today.
Judy Oh super. (*She kisses him*) Oh that's terrific.
Colin Now that I've got it I have to admit I was keen to get it.

Judy unwraps the parcel

I didn't know what to buy. Elizabeth says I'm hopeless at choosing. I won't be offended if you don't like it—I mean, don't feel obliged to wear it.

In the parcel is a pendant

Judy It's super—I . . . Thank you very much. I . . .
Colin What?
Judy Nothing. It really is very nice. Well! Only a few more days as the assistant.
Colin Yes.
Judy And start the new term as principal.
Colin Yes.

There is a silence. Somehow the gift has spoilt the mood that was there before Judy.

Judy What?
Colin Would you come away with me?
Judy You mean for a week-end or something?
Colin No. For good. Come and live with me.
Judy Oh Colin. What about your family?
Colin They don't need me—I'm almost irrelevant to them. Only I have to know now, see? Because I'd have to decline the headmaster's job if you— if you came with me. I couldn't very well take over the job at the same time as I'd run off with a member of the staff, could I?
Judy Am I really worth giving up the job for?
Colin Yes! Since I've met you I've felt—well, "alive" is the only way to describe it. I feel I'm living for something—it's not just the sex, though that's marvellous—it's the music and being able to talk. I feel exactly the same as I did when I was first a student—when everything seemed exciting—you know.
Judy Mmm.
Colin I thought we could clear off together. Pack up and go. What you were saying the other week—about "just travelling for as long as possible"— I can't get it out of my mind. But with the two of us.
Judy Oh Colin. I'd love to—I really would—but the thing is—I'm probably going back to Robert.
Colin I thought . . .
Judy I saw him the other day—in the park with the kids—they didn't see me. He was coping—no more. The kids were taking advantage of him, they really were. I hadn't realized, but they're turning into real little shits—in

just the time I've been away. And I don't want that to happen—basically, they're nice kids. I have to go back.

Colin I thought you couldn't . . .

Judy Things between Robert and me will be just the same. But how could I go and live with you—go off to Europe with you, and have a wonderful time, knowing what's going on at home?

Colin He'll find someone else.

Judy Who? Some jolly spinster who'll gladly take them on because it's the only way she'll get a family? Or some other wretch who's been abandoned with three of her own. I've tried to fight it—not to admit it—but the old clichés keep returning . . . "for better for worse"; "you've made your bed, now you must lie on it"; "loyalty"; "duty". They all dance through my head night after night after night. There's no escape. I have to go back.

Pause

Colin What about us?

Judy You know as well as I do.

Colin We could still see each other.

Judy No.

Colin There's always school.

Judy Your first duty as headmaster will be to accept my resignation.

Colin But—

Judy I'll have to, won't I.

A silence.

Colin If you knew how much I'd thought about it. About us—it would be a new start—a new life. I had visions of us in somewhere like Kashmir—or Nepal—you know, one of those adventure holidays.

Judy It'd probably be the monsoon and we'd both have dysentery.

The doorbell rings. They leap out of bed

Who can that be at this time of night? Oh hell, not Robert.

Colin Oh no! (*He begins dressing frantically*)

The doorbell rings again

Judy Just a minute! (*She goes to the hatstand*) Oh—here, your raincoat. I remembered at last. (*She throws it on the bed*)

Colin Thanks. Oh! I meant to bring your book.

Judy Doesn't matter. (*She turns on the main lights*)

The doorbell rings again

Coming!

Judy exits

Colin finishes dressing and we now realize that he has been coming to Judy's in his jogging gear. Voices off are heard with Judy trying to prevent the visitor from coming in.

Judy (*off*) It's too late at night ...
Man (*off*) No, no.
Judy (*off*) I was in bed—asleep ...
Man (*off*) Now you're up—just for a bit ...
Judy (*off*) No!

Then Judy comes into the room with Reg, who has a carrier bag

Reg. He just "happened to be passing".
Reg (*slightly drunk*) And I happened to have a bottle of gin, so I thought
why not call in and say Hallo. (*To Colin*) Did you happen to be running
by?
Colin No. Yes. I really must be going.
Reg Don't go, don't go. Have a very quick drink and *then* go.
Judy No please don't go.
Reg Not very polite just to run into a lady's place and run out again. What .
is it? Some sort of staff meeting? No—if it were, Judy'd hardly be in her.
dressing-gown—(*he moves the top of the gown just a fraction*)

She shakes off his hand

—with nothing on underneath. Anyone'd think ... Colin, you haven't! Not
you and Judy! (*Delighted*) Well!
Colin Look Reg, it's not like that.
Reg Old Colin an adulterer! Congratulations old man on joining the least
exclusive club in the Western World.
Colin No. You don't ...
Reg Well, well, well. Oh, we must drink to this.

*During the following he takes a gin bottle from his bag and opens it. He finds
three glasses on the chest-of-drawers and pours into each. He hands one to Judy,
who turns away, then to Colin, who takes it reluctantly, and puts it down. Lastly
Reg pours a drink for himself*

Colin Listen Reg, you don't understand.
Reg Oh, I understand all right. I understand. Who better. Very happy for you
both. I'm very pleased. I am. Very pleased. It is the first time, I take it—
I mean she is your first outside the—er—conjugal bonds? Unfair question.
Sure she is. Anyway. You'll find old man, now that you've broken your
duck, that the whole world of women suddenly opens up for you again—
just like it did once you'd had your first bit of nooky—remember? Once
you've endured the first deception, told the first lie, survived the first hours
of sleepless guilt—once you've done all that—you'll find you can live with
it surprisingly well. There's a ton of women out there waiting for you—
waiting to be cuddled and cosseted, to be made to feel important, to be
made love to—they're just like us—they want excitement, too. You'll soon
learn to spot them—teeny sexual hints in conversation; an over-willingness
to laugh; bright eyes and desperate mouths—they're all out there. Of course,
every now and then there's a bit of agony—one party falls for the other

and gets rejected when things get serious—you won't have been through all that of course—but by and large, taking it all in all, weighing it all up, the treadmill you've just got on—is just worth it.

Pause

Judy Reg, I wish you would go.

Reg I was faithful to Isobel for eight years. Scrupulous. Turned down offers from students—only two—mustn't exaggerate—refused offers from infant mistresses at refresher courses—once said no to a stout party at a hotel in Harrogate. And then it occurred to me that I was preserving my fidelity cherry so to speak. I was denying myself, for something Isobel didn't really enjoy. She doesn't. Oh she's done her fighting cats impersonation a couple of times, but given the choice between, say, her spinning wheel or—getting it regular—there was no question which she would choose.

Colin Come on Reg.

Reg You ever been placed second to a spinning wheel? Anyway, when I *realized*, when it dawned on me, that was the case—there seemed little point in hanging back. So ...

Colin Reg! (*He picks up his raincoat*)

Reg What, old man?

Colin Could you give me a lift home—I'm running late.

Reg Yes, you are, aren't you. Oh, I see! Yes, yes, get you home before Elizabeth begins to fret.

Colin She's out.

Reg Perfect.

Colin But she'll ...

Reg But she'll be in soon. Quite understand. Don't worry old man—you know me—soul of indiscretion—get you home in time. Well, well, well.

Colin So if you don't mind.

Reg Not at all. Not at all. (*To Judy, giving her the bottle and glass*) "Farewell my lovely." Just reading it. Good old Chandler—opiate of the masses.

Reg exits to the hallway

Colin turns, and he and Judy kiss

Judy I'm sorry.

The Lights fade, as—

the CURTAIN *falls*

SCENE 10

The dinner party continued

Reg, Robert, Isobel and Elizabeth are sitting in silence. Only Reg is eating his sweet—all the others are untouched. Reg finishes it

Reg That was delicious. (*There is no reply. He reaches for Isobel's and begins eating that*) It won't keep.

Colin enters with a pot of coffee and coffee cups and puts it on the coffee-table ready to serve—but he never gets round to serving it

Still no-one talks

(*Rising and sitting in the swivel chair*) Oh come on, everybody—it's not the end of the world. Every year in this country sixteen thousand kids get born to girls under eighteen—we have to build over twenty new schools a year for the little bastards. Sixteen thousand! That's over forty a day. Right now throughout the country, this scene is being repeated in forty other homes— eighty, if the fathers confess. For a tragedy it's a bit of a commonplace.

Colin You mean like "Two hundred killed in Peru landslide".

Reg Er—well.

Colin Not so hot if you're in the landslide.

Judy enters

Judy It sounds pretty definite, I'm afraid.

Elizabeth Oh.

Judy But obviously she'll go to the doctor and find out for certain. She— she wasn't up to facing you tonight. I said you'd understand.

Elizabeth Yes. Not that I do.

Judy Anyway, we must go.

Robert Yes. (*He rises*)

Elizabeth Oh don't go—please don't go. There's still the coffee. Please.

Judy All right. But we can't be late. We promised the baby-sitter ...

Judy and Robert sit. A silence

Elizabeth I was afraid this might happen. When she was young I almost used to hope that she'd grow up unattractive. And then one day a boy—he was a young man really, that's what made it worse—looked at Jane—sexually. I remember I hardly slept that night I was so worried—silly. And all her first dates—I was scared, you know—and I though she'd survived all that, that somehow now it would be all right.

Reg You should've put her on the pill.

Elizabeth How! How do you suggest to your own daughter that she go on the pill? It would be like saying we approved—like giving her a licence to go to bed with boys. I had no idea she was—no idea at all!

Colin They know all about these things. They get told at school.

Judy When?

Colin Er—sixth form usually. But they pick it up long before then.

Reg Yes, I told Stephen all about it years ago—fat lot of good it did when the time came. Colin, you'll have to put up a notice outside the school like they do in factories—you know, "There have been no accidents in this building for twenty-seven days", only yours'll say, "There have been no pregnancies in this school for so many days". Get a bit of school spirit into the thing.

Colin I'll have to do something.

Elizabeth But it's too late isn't it—in our case, it's too late.

Isobel I don't want them to get married.

Elizabeth But ...

Isobel Stephen's too young. He's got too much to do. Elizabeth, I'm terribly desperately sorry for what he's done, but I don't want him to get married. I'll pay the maintenance myself or whatever, but I don't want him tied down.

Reg What if they want to get married? Lots of kids their age get married these days—they cope.

Isobel He just sees young men with long hair pushing prams and thinks it's romantic. He doesn't see them cooped up in bed-sitters with the baby's crying driving them frantic. I'm sorry, but I'm not having Stephen married at seventeen.

Elizabeth She was doing so well at school. She was going to be a doctor.

Colin She could actually—er—wait a year before going to Medical School, and when the baby comes—decide—whether to—em—or keep it, you know.

A short silence

Judy Does she have to have the baby?

Elizabeth You mean an abortion?

Judy Yes.

Isobel We'd pay half.

Elizabeth I don't know—it's horrible, the very thought—of her ...

Robert And it's wrong.

Reg What?

Robert It's wrong. Abortion is wrong. It's killing human beings.

Reg Oh come on!

Robert It was wrong of them to have sex in the first place, but nobody ever tells kids *anything's* wrong these days. Parents are made to feel guilty even mentioning the word. But that doesn't mean she should have an abortion.

Reg Hell's teeth, are you a Catholic or something? How's all that going to help things?

Robert Abortion isn't the answer.

Reg It is! (*Rising*) It's almost the perfect answer. A few minutes unpleasantness and you've prevented two—and probably three—lives from being ruined. Don't tell me it's not the answer.

Robert (*rising*) All I'm saying is it's no way out of one wrong to commit another. Can't you see that it's people like you with your total lack of standards that've probably encouraged them to get into the situation they're in. What sort of example are you setting your students? You have affairs with girls who are too young to know any better. You treat your wife as though she were a piece of shit. You ...

Reg Listen, you smug, tax-evading prick, you wait until you find yourself in a similar position and see how you like it on your high horse.

Robert I've got too much sense to get myself into that position. (*He sits*)

Reg Oh, have you. Colin here and your wife have been leaping between the sheets for the last couple of months. Did you know that? So what if Judy was pregnant as a result—what would you say then to a quick trip to Harley Street? (*He sits*)

Pause

Judy To set everybody's mind at rest about one thing—I'm not pregnant.

Another silence

I'm sorry, Elizabeth—sorry that you found out, anyway. And I can assure you that it's all over.

Robert I suppose that's why you came back—because it finished.

Judy No! No it wasn't.

Elizabeth How could you! How could you come home and look me in the eye.

Colin You were usually asleep when I got home, which helped. Elizabeth— there's nothing I can say. It's all over as Judy says—it's happened—forget it.

Elizabeth How can I forget it!

Reg You'll get used to it Elizabeth. Look at Isobel, she doesn't care. It makes no difference to her.

Isobel It does! He thinks it doesn't because I've learned to live with it. But don't let him say I don't care.

Elizabeth What I can't understand is why. I do everything for you—I try to keep a nice house—why would you want to go to someone else? Even my own daughter prefers her to me. What have I done?

Colin Nothing, Elizabeth. It wasn't your fault—it wasn't anybody's—it was just one of those things that happened. Let's leave it at that for now. (*He rises and moves away*)

Judy (*rising to Reg*) Did you have to tell people. Did you have to?

Reg I can't stand that sort of sanctimonious right-wing clap-trap he's been talking all evening.

Judy So that's a good enough reason to hurt someone.

Reg (*rising*) Don't worry, he's bound to forgive you, when you'd probably much rather he gave you a black eye.

Robert I'd rather give you a black eye.

Isobel Oh do—oh please do!

Reg Come on! Come on!

Judy We really should be going.

Robert Yes.

Isobel (*rising*) Yes, we must, too.

Elizabeth Oh, the coffee!

Robert No, really.

Isobel picks up her bag: the handle breaks and it falls to the floor. She dissolves into tears

Isobel Damn, it was the first one I'd made.

Reg And she complains about the quality of manufactured goods!

Isobel Damn! (*She turns away up stage*)

Elizabeth I'll get your coats.

Elizabeth exits to the hall

Colin Well—enjoy the Greek islands.
Robert Thank you. Good luck ... with the job.
Colin Thanks.

Elizabeth enters with Judy's and Robert's coats, and Isobel's shawl, and hands them round

Robert Thank you for the evening.
Elizabeth Thank you for coming—it's been a lovely ...
Isobel Elizabeth—we'll get together—about the children—"children"! hah!—and try to decide, you know—what's best.
Elizabeth Yes, yes.
Isobel And thank you for tonight. We must have you back before long.
Reg Sorry about ...
Colin Too late for that Reg. It's done now, isn't it. (*He picks up the "Railway" book from the cupboard*)
Elizabeth I'll see you out.
Isobel Good night, Colin.
Robert Good night.
Colin Good night.

Isobel, Robert, Elizabeth and Reg exit to the hall, Reg without any "good night"

Judy (*following*) 'Bye.
Colin (*giving the book to Judy*) I hope you make it one day.
Judy I hope you ...

Judy exits

Colin sits on the sofa and pours himself a cup of coffee. He reaches for the sugar from habit, then stops, remembering that he has given it up. Then he deliberately puts two spoonfuls into his cup

Elizabeth comes into the room and sits on the sofa beside Colin without a word

Colin Would you like some coffee?

She shakes her head. A silence

Elizabeth What do we do now?
Colin What we do now, Elizabeth ... is the dishes.
The Lights fade, as—

the CURTAIN *falls*

FURNITURE AND PROPERTY LIST

The stage directions in the text fit the arrangements of furniture given in the ground plans below. How the inset scenes are arranged will depend on the size of the stage. (In the London production, a revolve was used)

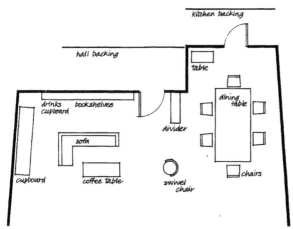

The sitting-room

On stage: Cupboard. *On it: Railway Bazaar* book, ashtray. *On wall above:* mirror. *On floor beside it:* wastepaper-basket.

Drinks cabinet. *In it:* gin, whisky, Drambuie, tonic water, sherry. *On shelf below:* tray with 6 wine glasses, tray with 6 tumblers, 6 sherry glasses, 3 wine glasses, 3 liqueur glasses, ice bucket, corkscrew, dish of lemon slices, cassette radio & cassettes.

Bookcase. *In it:* various books including 2 Art books, *Daisy Rothschild* book

Divider unit. *On it:* telephone, address book, diary, pencil, ashtray, matches

Small table. *On it:* hotplate, plant

Dining-table. *On it:* 6 table mats, 6 side plates, 6 knives, forks and soup spoons

6 dining chairs around table

Swivel chair. *On it:* "nurse" doll, cushion

Sofa. *On it:* cushions

Coffee-table. *On it:* ashtray, dish of olives

Off stage: Tray with plates of nuts, crackers, etc. **(Elizabeth)**
Box containing new clothes **(Colin)**
Bottle of red wine **(Colin)**
2 ice cubes **(Colin)**
Bottle of opened white wine **(Colin)**

Personal: **Isobel:** handbag with detachable handle, cigarettes, lighter
Judy: pendant
Colin: watch
Reg: watch

SCENE 2

The sitting-room

Strike: 2 wine bottles
Dirty glasses
Dishes of olives, etc.
Daisy and *Railway* books
Everything from dining-table

Set: Chairs into dining-table
4 letters on sofa
2 letters on coffee-table

Off stage: Briefcase containing school reports, pen, papers, wrapped copy of *5BX* book **(Colin)**

SCENE 3

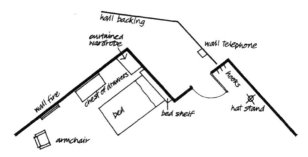

The bed-sitter

On stage: Bed with bedding roughly made, 2 cushions
Bookcase above bed. *On it:* Books, including *Railway Bazaar*
Chest-of-drawers. *On it:* 4 tumblers, record player, records
Small armchair
Hanging bookcase with books
Curtained wardrobe. *On top:* suitcases
Hatstand
In hall: wall telephone

Off stage: 2 mugs of coffee **(Judy)**

SCENE 4

The sitting-room

Strike: Reports, briefcase, pen
Letters
5BX book
Letters from wastepaper-basket
Whisky glasses

Set: *On dining-table:* 6 table mats, 6 wooden bowls & salad, 6 wooden plates, knives and forks, 6 *fondue* forks on plates, salad bowl with salad and servers, cruet, 6 wine glasses and wine, 4 wine bottles—2 red and 2 white, 6 napkins, 4 sauce dishes, *fondue* bowl on stand
Tray on small table
Telephone off hook
Railway and *Daisy* books as end of Scene 1

Off stage: Spare tray **(Elizabeth)**

SCENE 5

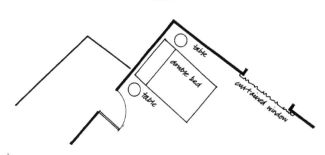

The bedroom

On stage: Double bed with bedding & duvet. *On it: Woman's Journal*
2 bedside tables. *On* **Elizabeth's:** lamp, face cream, box of tissues, alarm clock. *On* **Colin's:** lamp, nasal spray, *5BX* book, *Railway Bazaar* book

Off stage: Box of tissues **(Colin)**

SCENE 6

The bed-sitter

Strike: 2 mugs
Raincoat

Set: Pile of woman's clothes on floor by chair
Judy's shoes from Scene 3 on top of clothes
Judy's bag on armchair
2 cushions from bed on armchair

SCENE 7

The sitting-room

Strike: Any remaining *fondue* items
            Tray from small table

Set: 6 sweet spoons on dining-table
            Ashtray on dining-table
            Bottle of white wine on coffee-table
            Reg's glass on coffee-table
            Robert's glass, with wine, on dining-table

Check: *On dining-table:* table mats, napkins, 5 glasses, 2 wine bottles

Off stage: 6 dessert helpings (**Elizabeth**)

Personal: **Robert:** cigarettes, lighter

SCENE 8

The sitting-room

Strike: Everything from dining-table
            All wine bottles & glasses
            Railway and *Daisy* books

Set: Dining chairs into table
            Tray with coffee-pot, sugar bowl, milk jug, 1 cup, saucer & spoon on coffee-
               table
            House and Garden on coffee-table
            Evening Standard sheets & pencil on floor by coffee-table
            Evening Standard sheets in swivel chair
            1 cup, saucer & spoon on floor by swivel chair
            Briefcase on floor by swivel chair. *In it:* wrapped box of chocolates
            Colin's shoes by sofa

SCENE 9

The bed-sitter

Strike: Pile of woman's clothing
            2 cushions

Set: **Colin's** old raincoat on hatstand
            Pendant present behind armchair
            Janet Baker LP record box open on chair
            Libretto on bed
            Second pile of woman's clothing by chair
            Colin's tracksuit and plimsolls behind chair

Off stage: Carrier bag with gin bottle (**Reg**)

SCENE 10

The sitting-room

Strike: 2 liqueur glasses
            Coffee tray with cups etc.
            Newspaper
            Parcel
            Briefcase
            House and Garden

Set: *On dining-table:* table mats, 4 false sweets, 2 real sweets, 6 napkins, 6 sweet
          spoons, 6 glasses, 2 wine bottles
          Daisy book on coffee-table
          Railway book on cupboard
          Bottle of white wine on coffee-table
          6 chairs roughly round table

Check: **Isobel's** trick bag on sofa

Off stage: Pot of coffee, 6 cups, saucers, spoons, cream jug, sugar basin **(Colin)**
          Judy's coat, **Robert's** coat, **Isobel's** shawl **(Elizabeth)**

LIGHTING PLOT

Property fittings required: wall brackets (sitting-room,) 2 matching bed lamps (bed-room), small table lamp, bedside lamp, pendant (bed-sitter)
3 interiors: a sitting-room, a bedroom, a bed-sitter

Scene 1

To open:	Wall brackets and full interior lighting on	
Cue 1:	**Colin:** "... Social Club Welwyn." (He sits) *Fade to Black-out*	(Page 9)

SCENE 2

To open:	As Scene 1	
Cue 2:	As **Colin** does exercises *Fade to Black-out*	(Page 13)

SCENE 3

To open:	Dim interior lighting	
Cue 3:	**Judy** switches on main light *Snap on pendant*	(Page 14)
Cue 4:	As **Colin** and **Judy** exit *Fade to Black-out*	(Page 17)

SCENE 4

To open:	As Scene 1	
Cue 5:	**Reg:** "... to shut up about that." *Fade to Black-out*	(Page 21)

SCENE 5

To open:	Both bedside lamps on	
Cue 6:	**Elizabeth** turns out her bedlamp *Snap out bed lamp and covering spots*	(Page 22)
Cue 7:	**Colin** lies back in bed *Fade to Black-out*	(Page 23)

SCENE 6

To open:	Both bedsitter lamps on	
Cue 8:	**Judy** kisses **Colin** *Fade to Black-out*	(Page 26)

Scene 7

To open: As Scene 1

Cue 9 :   **Reg:** "The bloody little fools."   (Page 30)
            Fade to Black-out

Scene 8

To open: As Scene 1

Cue 10 : **Elizabeth** reads magazine   (Page 34)
            Fade to Black-out

Scene 9

To open: Small bed-sitter lamp on

Cue 11 : **Judy** switches on bedside lamp   (Page 34)
            Snap on lamp and covering spots

Cue 12 : **Judy** turns on main light   (Page 36)
            Snap on pendant

Cue 13 : **Judy:** "I'm sorry."   (Page 38)
            Fade to Black-out

Scene 10

To open: As Scene 1

Cue 14 : **Colin:** "... is ... the dishes."   (Page 42)
            Fade to Black-out

EFFECTS PLOT

Cue 1:	**Elizabeth** places book on coffee-table *Toilet flushes*	(Page 1)
Cue 2:	**Elizabeth:** "No, thank you." *Door chimes*	(Page 5)

SCENE 2

Cue 3:	**Elizabeth** goes towards phone *Phone rings*	(Page 10)
Cue 4:	**Elizabeth:** "... *don't* leave it too late." (2nd time) *Phone rings—twice only*	(Page 12)

SCENE 3

No cues

SCENE 4

No cues

SCENE 5

No cues

SCENE 6

No cues

SCENE 7

No cues

SCENE 8

Cue 5:	**Colin** and **Elizabeth** exchange papers *Telephone rings*	(Page 31)
Cue 6:	**Elizabeth** replaces phone on hook *Loud rock music: reduce to $\frac{1}{4}$ after Colin goes out to protest:* *fade altogether when he returns and shuts door*	(Page 31)
Cue 7:	After **Colin** exits *Front door slams*	(Page 34)
Cue 8:	When ready *Phone rings*	(Page 34)

SCENE 9

Cue 9:	As Scene opens *Record of Janet Baker in "The Dream of Gerontius"—con-* *tinue to end of side*	(Page 34)

Cue 10:	**Judy:** "... we'd both have dysentery." *Doorbell rings*	(Page 36)
Cue 11:	**Colin:** "Oh no!" *Doorbell rings*	(Page 36)
Cue 12:	**Judy** turns on main lights *Doorbell rings*	(Page 36)

SCENE 10

No cues